www.thequitegoodcompany.com

30 Essential Algorithms in Python

By Zara Loop

Quite
GOOD BOOKS

www.thequitegoodcompany.com

Welcome to „30 Essential Algorithms in Python"!

This book is designed to be a comprehensive guide to some of the most important algorithms in the field of computer science. Whether you are a student, a software professional, or a coding enthusiast, this book aims to enrich your understanding of these fundamental algorithms and illustrate how they form the backbone of modern computing.

Who This Book Is For

This book is intended for readers with a basic understanding of programming, especially in Python. The algorithms are explained in Python for practical understanding and implementation. Whether you are beginning your journey in computer science or looking to brush up on your algorithmic skills, this book offers valuable insights and examples.

Setting Up Your Python Environment

To get the most out of this book, you will need a working Python environment. Python 3.x is recommended for its latest features and support. You can download and install Python from the official website and choose an Integrated Development Environment (IDE) like PyCharm, Jupyter Notebook, or even a simple text editor like VSCode or Sublime Text for writing and executing your code.

Additional Python Packages

Some algorithms may require additional Python packages for optimal implementation. These packages can be easily installed using Python's package manager, pip. For example, you might need to install NumPy for numerical operations, which can be done using the command pip install numpy in your command line interface.

Tips for Success

Testing and Debugging: Regularly test and debug the algorithms with different inputs to deepen your understanding.
Experimentation: Feel free to modify the code examples and observe how these changes affect the algorithm's performance.
Further Learning: This book is a step in your learning journey. Explore additional resources like advanced books, online courses, and community forums to further expand your knowledge.

Embarking on Your Journey

As you turn the pages, remember that mastering algorithms is a journey. Each chapter is a step forward in this exciting path. Enjoy your journey through the fascinating world of algorithms, and may this book be a valuable companion on your way to becoming a proficient problem-solver and programmer!

01 QuickSort

Introduction and Historical Background

QuickSort is a highly efficient sorting algorithm and is based on the divide-and-conquer principle. It was developed by Tony Hoare in 1960 while he was a visiting student at Moscow State University. QuickSort has become one of the most widely used sorting methods due to its efficiency in handling large datasets.

Explanation and Theory

Conceptual Explanation:
QuickSort works by selecting a ‚pivot' element from the array and partitioning the other elements into two sub-arrays, according to whether they are less than or greater than the pivot. The sub-arrays are then sorted recursively. This can be done in-place, requiring small additional amounts of memory to perform the sorting.

Mathematical Foundation:
The efficiency of QuickSort is highly dependent on the choice of the pivot. In the worst case, it has a time complexity of $O(n^2)$, but with a good pivot, the average time complexity is $O(n \log n)$.

Use Cases and Applications

Real-World Applications:
QuickSort is used in various applications due to its efficiency and ease of implementation. It's particularly effective for large datasets and is used in systems where time efficiency is critical, such as database sorting and search algorithms.

Case Studies or Examples:
A common use case is in the implementation of sorting functions in standard libraries of various programming languages like Python's sorted() function.

Python Implementation:

```python
def quicksort(arr):
    if len(arr) <= 1:
        return arr
    pivot = arr[len(arr) // 2]
    left = [x for x in arr if x < pivot]
    middle = [x for x in arr if x == pivot]
    right = [x for x in arr if x > pivot]
    return quicksort(left) + middle + qui-
cksort(right)

# Example usage
arr = [3, 6, 8, 10, 1, 2, 1]
print(quicksort(arr))
```

This Python implementation of QuickSort shows its recursive nature and how it partitions the array. The code is simple and demonstrates the basic concept of the algorithm.

02 MergeSort

Introduction and Historical Background

MergeSort is a classic example of the divide-and-conquer strategy in algorithms. It was invented by John von Neumann in 1945. This algorithm is known for its efficiency in sorting large lists or arrays and is used in various applications, including sorting large databases.
Explanation and Theory

Conceptual Explanation:
MergeSort divides the array into halves, sorts each half, and then merges the sorted halves back together. Initially, it divides the list into the smallest unit (1 element), then compares each element with the adjacent list to sort and merge them back to the larger list. The process is repeated until the whole list is merged and sorted.

Mathematical Foundation:
MergeSort guarantees a time complexity of O(n log n) in the worst, average, and best cases, making it more predictable than algorithms like QuickSort, especially for datasets where the worst-case scenario is a concern.

Use Cases and Applications

Real-World Applications:
MergeSort is particularly useful in situations where predictable performance is critical. It is often used in systems where stability (the order of equal elements is preserved) is necessary. For instance, MergeSort is used in external sorting (sorting data that doesn't fit into memory).

Case Studies or Examples:
An example is sorting a large number of records stored in files, where MergeSort can efficiently handle the sorting by dividing and merging the records without loading everything into memory.

Python Implementation:

```python
def merge_sort(arr):
    if len(arr) > 1:
        mid = len(arr) // 2
        L = arr[:mid]
        R = arr[mid:]

        merge_sort(L)
        merge_sort(R)

        i = j = k = 0

        while i < len(L) and j < len(R):
            if L[i] < R[j]:
                arr[k] = L[i]
                i += 1
            else:
                arr[k] = R[j]
                j += 1
            k += 1

        while i < len(L):
            arr[k] = L[i]
            i += 1
            k += 1

        while j < len(R):
```

```python
            arr[k] = R[j]
            j += 1
            k += 1

# Example usage
arr = [12, 11, 13, 5, 6, 7]
merge_sort(arr)
print(f"Sorted array is: {arr}")
```

This Python code demonstrates the divide-and-conquer approach of Merge-Sort, showing how the list is divided and merged in a sorted manner.

03 HeapSort

Introduction and Historical Background

HeapSort is a comparison-based sorting technique based on the binary heap data structure. It was developed by J. W. J. Williams in 1964. HeapSort is notable for its ability to sort data with minimal space requirements and is particularly efficient for priority-queue implementations.
Explanation and Theory

Conceptual Explanation:
HeapSort organizes the array into a heap, usually a max heap, where the largest element is placed at the root of the heap. It then swaps the root (largest element) with the last item of the heap followed by reducing the size of the heap by one. The process is repeated until the heap is reduced to one element. During this process, the array gets sorted.

Mathematical Foundation:
HeapSort has a time complexity of $O(n \log n)$ for both the worst and average cases, similar to MergeSort. Its performance largely depends on the height of the tree, leading to its log n component in complexity.

Use Cases and Applications

Real-World Applications:
HeapSort is particularly effective in scenarios where complete sorting of an array is necessary, especially when additional memory usage needs to be minimized. It's widely used in systems where time and space efficiency is

critical, like embedded systems or operating systems.

Case Studies or Examples:
A practical example is in the implementation of efficient priority queues,
which are used in scheduling processes in operating systems or in pathfinding algorithms like Dijkstra's algorithm.

Python Implementation:

```python
def heapify(arr, n, i):
    largest = i
    l = 2 * i + 1
    r = 2 * i + 2

    if l < n and arr[i] < arr[l]:
        largest = l

    if r < n and arr[largest] < arr[r]:
        largest = r

    if largest != i:
        arr[i], arr[largest] = arr[largest], arr[i]
        heapify(arr, n, largest)

def heapSort(arr):
    n = len(arr)

    for i in range(n // 2 - 1, -1, -1):
        heapify(arr, n, i)

    for i in range(n-1, 0, -1):
        arr[i], arr[0] = arr[0], arr[i]
        heapify(arr, i, 0)

# Example usage
arr = [12, 11, 13, 5, 6, 7]
heapSort(arr)
print(f"Sorted array is: {arr}")
```

This implementation shows the creation of the heap and the sorting process.
The code is a clear demonstration of how the heap properties are maintained

throughout the algorithm.

04 BubbleSort

Introduction and Historical Background

BubbleSort, also known as the sinking sort, is a simple sorting algorithm. This method is known for its simplicity and has been introduced to novice programmers as an educational tool. Despite its inefficiency on large lists, it remains popular due to its ease of understanding and implementation. Explanation and Theory

Conceptual Explanation:
BubbleSort repeatedly steps through the list, compares adjacent elements, and swaps them if they are in the wrong order. The pass through the list is repeated until the list is sorted. The algorithm gets its name because smaller elements „bubble" to the top of the list.

Mathematical Foundation:
Because it only uses comparisons to operate on elements, it is a comparison sort. In terms of complexity, BubbleSort is not suitable for large data sets as its average and worst-case complexity are both $O(n^2)$.
Use Cases and Applications

Real-World Applications:
While not used in practical applications due to its inefficiency, BubbleSort is often taught in introductory computer science courses to help students understand the basic concept of sorting algorithms. It's also occasionally used in cases where the dataset is almost sorted or extremely small.

Case Studies or Examples:
An example could be a small-scale, in-memory sorting for a few items where simplicity is more critical than efficiency, like sorting a small list of names or items in a non-performance-critical part of an application.

Python Implementation:

```python
def bubbleSort(arr):
    n = len(arr)
```

```python
    for i in range(n-1):
        for j in range(0, n-i-1):
            if arr[j] > arr[j+1]:
                arr[j], arr[j+1] = arr[j+1], arr[j]

# Example usage
arr = [64, 34, 25, 12, 22, 11, 90]
bubbleSort(arr)
print(„Sorted array is:“)
for i in range(len(arr)):
    print(„%d“ % arr[i], end=“ „)
```

This code snippet shows the simplicity of BubbleSort. It iterates over the array and swaps elements in place, reflecting the basic nature of the algorithm.

05 InsertionSort

Introduction and Historical Background

InsertionSort is a simple and efficient comparison sort algorithm that builds the final sorted array (or list) one item at a time. It is much less efficient on large lists than more advanced algorithms like QuickSort, HeapSort, or MergeSort. However, its simplicity makes it excellent for small datasets.

Explanation and Theory

Conceptual Explanation:
InsertionSort works by taking elements from the list one by one and inserting them into their correct position into a new sorted list. In arrays, the new list and the remaining elements can share the array's space, but insertion is expensive, requiring shifting all following elements over by one.

Mathematical Foundation:
The best-case time complexity for InsertionSort is $O(n)$, which occurs when the input array is already sorted. In the average and worst-case scenarios, its complexity is $O(n^2)$, making it inefficient for large datasets.

Use -Cases and Applications

Real-World Applications:
InsertionSort is used when there are relatively few elements to sort, or if
the array is mostly sorted to begin with. It's an excellent choice for small
to medium-sized lists and is often used in conjunction with more complex
algorithms.

Case Studies or Examples:
A common use case is in the implementation of more sophisticated sorting algorithms, like Timsort, where InsertionSort is used for sorting small
arrays.

Python Implementation:

```python
def insertionSort(arr):
    for i in range(1, len(arr)):
        key = arr[i]
        j = i-1
        while j >=0 and key < arr[j] :
                arr[j + 1] = arr[j]
                j -= 1
        arr[j + 1] = key

# Example usage
arr = [12, 11, 13, 5, 6]
insertionSort(arr)
for i in range(len(arr)):
    print („%d“ %arr[i], end=“ „)
```

This Python code illustrates the basic mechanism of InsertionSort - inserting
each element of the array into its proper place in the sorted part of the array.

06 SelectionSort

Introduction and Historical Background

SelectionSort is a straightforward and intuitive sorting algorithm. Although
it is not typically used for large datasets due to its inefficiency, its simplicity
makes it useful for teaching the basics of sorting theory and for scenarios

where the complexity of the data set is low.

Explanation and Theory

Conceptual Explanation:
SelectionSort works by repeatedly finding the minimum element from the unsorted part of the list and moving it to the beginning. This process continues moving the unsorted array boundary by one element to the right after each iteration.

Mathematical Foundation:
The time complexity of SelectionSort is $O(n^2)$ for all cases (best, average, and worst), as it always makes $n(n-1)/2$ comparisons, regardless of the initial order of the elements.

Use Cases and Applications

Real-World Applications:
SelectionSort is mainly used in educational settings to introduce students to the concept of sorting. However, it can be practical in cases where the simplicity of the algorithm is more important than efficiency, or when the dataset is small and mostly sorted.

Case Studies or Examples:
An example is sorting a small list of items in an environment with very limited system resources, where more complex algorithms may not be feasible.

Python Implementation:

```python
def selectionSort(arr):
    for i in range(len(arr)):
        min_idx = i
        for j in range(i+1, len(arr)):
            if arr[min_idx] > arr[j]:
                min_idx = j
        arr[i], arr[min_idx] = arr[min_idx], arr[i]

# Example usage
arr = [64, 25, 12, 22, 11]
selectionSort(arr)
print("Sorted array is:", arr)
```

This Python code provides a straightforward example of how SelectionSort iterates through the list, repeatedly selecting the smallest element to place at the start of the sorted section.

07 RadixSort

Introduction and Historical Background

RadixSort is a non-comparative integer sorting algorithm that sorts data with integer keys by grouping keys by individual digits which share the same significant position and value. It was first introduced in 1887 by Herman Hollerith as part of a tabulating machine and has evolved significantly since then.

Explanation and Theory

Conceptual Explanation:
RadixSort works on the basis of „digit by digit" sort starting from the least significant digit to the most significant digit. Radix sort uses counting sort as a subroutine to sort an array of numbers. Since it sorts digit by digit, it has a unique advantage in sorting numbers efficiently compared to other comparison-based sorting algorithms.

Mathematical Foundation:
RadixSort's time complexity is $O(nk)$ for n keys which have k digits. This makes it efficient for large datasets, particularly when the range of input values (k) is not significantly larger than the number of items being sorted (n).

Use Cases and Applications

Real-World Applications:
RadixSort is used in scenarios where the length of the integers (number of digits) is limited, such as telephone numbers, bank account numbers, or other large datasets of integers where the range is limited.

Case Studies or Examples:
A practical application of RadixSort can be seen in sorting large databases of numerical identifiers where the identifiers have a fixed number of digits.

Python Implementation:

```python
def countingSort(arr, exp1):
    n = len(arr)
    output = [0] * n
    count = [0] * 10

    for i in range(0, n):
        index = arr[i] // exp1
        count[index % 10] += 1

    for i in range(1, 10):
        count[i] += count[i - 1]

    i = n - 1
    while i >= 0:
        index = arr[i] // exp1
        output[count[index % 10] - 1] = arr[i]
        count[index % 10] -= 1
        i -= 1

    for i in range(0, len(arr)):
        arr[i] = output[i]

def radixSort(arr):
    max1 = max(arr)
    exp = 1
    while max1 / exp > 1:
        countingSort(arr, exp)
        exp *= 10

# Example usage
arr = [170, 45, 75, 90, 802, 24, 2, 66]
radixSort(arr)
print(„Sorted array is:“, arr)
```

This Python implementation of RadixSort demonstrates the process of sorting numbers digit by digit, leveraging a counting sort subroutine for each digit.

08 ShellSort

Introduction and Historical Background

ShellSort, also known as the diminishing increment sort, was introduced by Donald Shell in 1959. This algorithm is a generalization of insertion sort that allows the exchange of items that are far apart. ShellSort is an in-place comparison sort and is mainly important due to its efficiency with medium-sized lists, outperforming the more traditional insertion sort.

Explanation and Theory

Conceptual Explanation:
ShellSort works by comparing elements separated by a gap of several positions. This gap is reduced progressively with each pass, with the final pass being a simple insertion sort, but by this time, the list is already fairly sorted, making the final pass efficient. The essence of ShellSort is that it allows the exchange of items that are far apart, leading to a faster convergence to a sorted list.

Mathematical Foundation:
The time complexity of ShellSort varies based on the gap sequence used. In the worst-case scenario, its complexity can range from $O(n \log n)$ to $O(n^2)$, depending on the chosen gap sequence. However, no optimal gap sequence is known for the general case.

Use Cases and Applications

Real-World Applications:
ShellSort is particularly effective for medium-sized datasets or partially sorted arrays. Its implementation is simpler than more advanced sorting algorithms like QuickSort, making it a good choice for scenarios where simplicity and moderate efficiency are required.

Case Studies or Examples:
An example could be in embedded systems where memory and processing power are limited, and the dataset size doesn't justify the overhead of more complex algorithms.

Python Implementation:

```python
def shellSort(arr):
    n = len(arr)
    gap = n // 2

    while gap > 0:
        for i in range(gap, n):
            temp = arr[i]
            j = i
            while  j >= gap and arr[j - gap] > temp:
                arr[j] = arr[j - gap]
                j -= gap
            arr[j] = temp
        gap //= 2

# Example usage
arr = [12, 34, 54, 2, 3]
shellSort(arr)
print(„Sorted array is:", arr)
```

This implementation demonstrates the incremental approach of ShellSort, where the array is partially sorted with a decreasing gap until a final insertion sort pass is made.

09 CountingSort

Introduction and Historical Background

CountingSort is an integer sorting algorithm that is non-comparative and operates by counting the number of objects that have distinct key values. This type of sorting algorithm is often used for sorting elements with a specific range and works best when the range of potential values is not significantly greater than the number of elements to be sorted.

Explanation and Theory

Conceptual Explanation:
CountingSort calculates the number of occurrences of each distinct element

in the input, then places each element directly into its correct position in the output array. It essentially counts the occurrences of each value, then uses this count to position each element in its proper place.

Mathematical Foundation:
The time complexity of CountingSort is O(n + k), where n is the number of elements in the input array and k is the range of input. This makes it efficient when the range (k) is not significantly larger than the number of elements (n).

Use Cases and Applications
Real-World Applications:
CountingSort is particularly useful when sorting integers in a small range, such as ages, scores, or other discrete data sets. It's also used as a subroutine in more complex sorting algorithms like RadixSort for sorting digits.

Case Studies or Examples:
An example of its application is in sorting data like census information where the range of values (like age) is known to be limited.

Python Implementation:

```python
def countingSort(arr):
    max_val = max(arr)
    m = max_val + 1
    count = [0] * m

    for a in arr:
        count[a] += 1
    i = 0
    for a in range(m):
        for c in range(count[a]):
            arr[i] = a
            i += 1
    return arr

# Example usage
arr = [1
```

This Python code demonstrates the CountingSort algorithm, showcasing how the counts of each element are used to arrange them in sorted order.

10 Binary Search

Introduction and Historical Background

Binary Search is a classic algorithm in computer science. It was first documented in the mid-20th century, but its roots trace back to ancient methods for searching sorted lists. This algorithm is known for its efficiency in finding items in sorted lists and is a fundamental algorithm in the field of computing.

Explanation and Theory

Conceptual Explanation:
Binary Search is a search algorithm that finds the position of a target value within a sorted array. It compares the target value to the middle element of the array; if they are not equal, the half in which the target cannot lie is eliminated, and the search continues on the remaining half, again taking the middle element for comparison.

Mathematical Foundation:
The time complexity of Binary Search is $O(\log n)$, making it much more efficient than linear search, especially for large lists. The key requirement for Binary Search to work is that the data collection should be sorted.

Use Cases and Applications

Real-World Applications:
Binary Search is widely used in computing, from simple lookup operations in sorted arrays to more complex applications like finding the specific version where a software bug was introduced (in version control systems) or in database indexing.

Case Studies or Examples:
A common example is in searching for a word in a dictionary or a contact in a sorted contact list, where Binary Search efficiently narrows down the search area.

Python Implementation:

```python
def binarySearch(arr, target):
    low = 0
    high = len(arr) - 1

    while low <= high:
        mid = (low + high) // 2
        guess = arr[mid]
        if guess == target:
            return mid
        if guess > target:
            high = mid - 1
        else:
            low = mid + 1
    return None

# Example usage
arr = [1, 3, 5, 7, 9]
print(„Search for 5:“, binarySearch(arr, 5)) # Output: 2
```

This Python code provides a clear demonstration of how Binary Search locates a target value by iteratively dividing the search interval in half.

11 Depth-First Search (DFS)

Introduction and Historical Background

Depth-First Search (DFS) is a fundamental algorithm used in graph theory to traverse or search through graph data structures. The concept of DFS emerged from tree data structure exploration methods and was later generalized to graphs. It is one of the cornerstones in various graph-related algorithms.

Explanation and Theory

Conceptual Explanation:
DFS explores as far as possible along each branch before backtracking. It

starts at a selected node (root if a tree), explores as far along the current branch as possible, and, upon reaching the end of the branch, backtracks to the last node that had unexplored paths and continues the search. DFS can be implemented using recursion or a stack.

Mathematical Foundation:
The time complexity of DFS is $O(V + E)$, where V is the number of vertices and E is the number of edges in the graph. This makes DFS suitable for exploring all the nodes and edges of a large graph efficiently.

Use Cases and Applications

Real-World Applications:
DFS is used in various areas including cycle detection in graphs, pathfinding algorithms, topological sorting in directed graphs, and solving puzzles with only one solution, such as mazes.

Case Studies or Examples:
A practical example is in network analysis, like mapping routes in a network or finding if a network is cyclic.

Python Implementation:

```python
def dfs(graph, node, visited):
    if node not in visited:
        visited.append(node)
        for neighbour in graph[node]:
            dfs(graph, neighbour, visited)
    return visited


# Example usage
graph = {
    ‚A‘ : [‚B‘, ‘C‘],
    ‚B‘ : [‚D‘, ‚E‘],
    ‚C‘ : [‚F‘],
    ‚D‘ : [],
    ‚E‘ : [‚F‘],
    ‚F‘ : []
}
visited = dfs(graph, ‘A‘, [])
print(„DFS order:“, visited) # Output: [‚A‘, ‚B‘,
```

‚D', ‚E', ‚F', ‚C']

This Python code snippet demonstrates DFS in a simple graph structure, showing how it traverses through all the nodes by diving deeper before moving to a neighboring node.

12 Breadth-First Search (BFS)
Introduction and Historical Background

Breadth-First Search (BFS) is a fundamental algorithm in graph theory for traversing or searching through the nodes of a graph. It explores the neighbor nodes at the present depth prior to moving on to the nodes at the next depth level. BFS was first introduced by Konrad Zuse in 1945 in a slightly different form and has since become a staple in graph algorithm theory.

Explanation and Theory

Conceptual Explanation:
BFS starts at a specific ‚source' node and explores all its neighboring nodes. Then, for each of these nearest nodes, it explores their unvisited neighbors and so on, until it covers all the nodes in the graph. BFS uses a queue data structure to manage the order in which nodes are visited and explored.

Mathematical Foundation:
The time complexity of BFS is $O(V + E)$, where V is the number of vertices and E is the number of edges in the graph. This makes it particularly effective for searching in graphs where the path lengths from the source to all vertices are comparatively short.

Use Cases and Applications

Real-World Applications:
BFS is used in many areas, including finding the shortest path in unweighted graphs, level order traversal in trees, and in algorithms for finding connected components in undirected graphs.

Case Studies or Examples:
A common application is in social networking platforms for finding the shortest path between two people, representing the degrees of separation.

Python Implementation:

```python
from collections import deque

def bfs(graph, start):
    visited, queue = set(), deque([start])
    while queue:
        vertex = queue.popleft()
        if vertex not in visited:
            visited.add(vertex)
            queue.extend(set(graph[vertex]) - visited)
    return visited

# Example usage
graph = {0: [1, 2], 1: [2], 2: [3], 3: [1,2]}
print(„BFS order:", bfs(graph, 0)) # Output: {0, 1, 2, 3}
```

This Python code snippet demonstrates BFS in a graph, showing how it explores nodes level by level using a queue.

13 Linear Search

Introduction and Historical Background

Linear Search or sequential search is one of the simplest searching algorithms. As its name implies, it checks each element of the list sequentially until the desired element is found or the list ends. This method is straightforward and requires no additional data structures or algorithms, making it a basic but essential concept in computer science.

Explanation and Theory

Conceptual Explanation:
Linear Search works by starting at the beginning of a list and checking each element one by one for the target value. If the target is found, the search stops and returns the index of the element. If the list does not contain the target, the search returns an indication that the value is not present.

Mathematical Foundation:
The time complexity of Linear Search is O(n), where n is the number of elements in the list. This means that, in the worst case, it checks each element once. This simplicity makes it useful for small, unsorted datasets.

Use Cases and Applications

Real-World Applications:
Linear Search is mostly used when dealing with small or unsorted datasets where the overhead of more complex algorithms is not justified. It's also used in situations where the data is streaming or when the dataset is too large to be sorted.

Case Studies or Examples:
An example is finding a specific name in an unsorted list of participants in a small-scale event or searching for a particular file in an unorganized file system.

Python Implementation:

```python
def linearSearch(arr, target):
    for i in range(len(arr)):
        if arr[i] == target:
            return i
    return -1

# Example usage
arr = [23, 48, 19, 7, 86, 42]
target = 19
print(f"Element found at index: {linearSearch(arr,
target)}") # Output: 2
```

This Python code demonstrates a basic Linear Search, iterating through each element until the target is found or the end of the list is reached.

14 A* Search

Introduction and Historical Background

A* Search (pronounced „A-star") is a pathfinding and graph traversal algorithm widely used in computer science. It was first created in the 1960s as part of AI (Artificial Intelligence) research. A* is notable for its effectiveness in finding the shortest path and for its ability to combine the strengths of Dijkstra's Algorithm and Greedy Best-First-Search.

Explanation and Theory

Conceptual Explanation:
A* Search finds the least-cost path from a given start node to a target node. It uses a heuristic to estimate the cost to reach the target from each node, combining this with the cost to reach the node from the start. This makes it a best-first search algorithm that prioritizes paths that seem to be leading closer to the target.

Mathematical Foundation:
The efficiency of A* Search depends on the heuristic. The time complexity can vary widely but is generally efficient for many practical applications. A* is optimally efficient for any given consistent heuristic, meaning that it examines fewer nodes than any other algorithm with the same heuristic.

Use Cases and Applications

Real-World Applications:
A* is used in various fields, including AI for games and robotics, network routing, and in GIS (Geographical Information Systems) for finding the shortest path.

Case Studies or Examples:
In video games, A* is used to calculate paths for characters to move between points efficiently, avoiding obstacles and considering terrain costs.

Python Implementation:

```python
import heapq

def astar_search(graph, start, end, h):
    open_set = set(start)
    closed_set = set()
    g = {start: 0}
    parents = {start: start}
    pq = [(h(start), start)]
```

```python
    while open_set:
        current = heapq.heappop(pq)[1]
        if current == end:
            path = []
            while parents[current] != current:
                path.append(current)
                current = parents[current]
            path.append(start)
            return path[::-1]
        open_set.remove(current)
        closed_set.add(current)
        for node in graph[current]:
            if node in closed_set:
                continue
            tentative_g_score = g[current] + gra-
ph[current][node]
            if node not in open_set or tentative_g_
score < g[node]:
                open_set.add(node)
                heapq.heappush(pq, (tentative_g_
score + h(node), node))
                parents[node] = current
                g[node] = tentative_g_score
    return None

# Example usage
def heuristic(n):
    H = {
        ,A': 1,
        ,B': 1,
        ,C': 1,
        ,D': 1
    }
    return H[n]

graph = {
    ,A': {,B': 1, ,C': 3},
    ,B': {,D': 1},
    ,C': {,D': 1},
    ,D': {}
```

```
}

path = astar_search(graph, ,A', ,D', heuristic)
print("Path found:", path)
```

This Python implementation of A* demonstrates how it combines the heuristic and the actual cost to find the most efficient path from a start to an end node.

15 Dijkstra's Algorithm

Introduction and Historical Background

Dijkstra's Algorithm is a well-known algorithm for finding the shortest path between nodes in a graph, which may represent, for example, road networks. It was conceived by computer scientist Edsger W. Dijkstra in 1956 and published three years later. The algorithm is famous for its efficiency and is a classic example in teaching computer science and graph theory.

Explanation and Theory

Conceptual Explanation:
Dijkstra's Algorithm works by iteratively picking the vertex with the minimum distance from the start vertex, updating the distance of its adjacent vertices, and continuing this process until all vertices have been processed. It's known for its ability to find the shortest path in a graph with non-negative edge weights.

Mathematical Foundation:
The time complexity of Dijkstra's Algorithm can vary depending on the implementation. With a simple linear array, the complexity is $O(V^2)$, where V is the number of vertices. However, with a priority queue, it can be reduced to $O(V + E \log V)$, making it more suitable for larger graphs.

Use Cases and Applications

Real-World Applications:
Dijkstra's Algorithm is widely used in network routing protocols, for mapping and navigation systems to find the shortest path between two points, and in various fields like telecommunications for network routing.

Case Studies or Examples:
An example of its application is in GPS systems for finding the shortest driving route to a destination.

Python Implementation:

```python
import heapq

def dijkstra(graph, start):
    distances = {vertex: float(‚infinity‘) for vertex in graph}
    distances[start] = 0
    pq = [(0, start)]

    while pq:
        current_distance, current_vertex = heapq.heappop(pq)

        if current_distance > distances[current_vertex]:
            continue

        for neighbor, weight in graph[current_vertex].items():
            distance = current_distance + weight

            if distance < distances[neighbor]:
                distances[neighbor] = distance
                heapq.heappush(pq, (distance, neighbor))

    return distances

# Example usage
graph = {
    ‚A‘: {‚B‘: 1, ‚C‘: 4},
    ‚B‘: {‚A‘: 1, ‚C‘: 2, ‚D‘: 5},
    ‚C‘: {‚A‘: 4, ‚B‘: 2, ‚D‘: 1},
    ‚D‘: {‚B‘: 5, ‚C‘: 1}
}
```

```
print(dijkstra(graph, ‚A'))
```

This Python implementation of Dijkstra's Algorithm shows how it calculates the shortest path from a starting node to all other nodes in a weighted graph.

16 Greedy Best-First Search

Introduction and Historical Background

Greedy Best-First Search is a search algorithm that explores a graph by selecting the most promising node according to a specified heuristic. This algorithm is classified as a greedy algorithm because it picks the path which appears best at that moment, without considering the global context. It's a part of a family of algorithms used for searching and pathfinding in the field of artificial intelligence.

Explanation and Theory

Conceptual Explanation:
Greedy Best-First Search algorithm works by choosing the path that appears to be the most promising at each step. It makes this decision based on a heuristic that estimates how close the end of a path is to the target. The algorithm does not guarantee the shortest path, but it does often find a path close to the shortest one in less time than algorithms like A*.

Mathematical Foundation:
The time complexity of Greedy Best-First Search can vary greatly depending on the heuristic and the structure of the search space. Its performance is often better than that of simple algorithms like DFS or BFS, especially in cases with large graphs and dispersed goals.

Use Cases and Applications

Real-World Applications:
This algorithm is used in various pathfinding and graph traversal algorithms, especially in situations where finding an exact shortest path is less critical than finding an approximate path quickly.

Case Studies or Examples:
An example of its use is in AI for games, where it can be used to make decisi-

ons for non-player characters or agents in large environments where a quick decision is more beneficial than the absolute shortest path.

Python Implementation:

```python
import heapq

def greedy_best_first_search(graph, start, goal, h):
    visited = set()
    queue = [(h(start), start)]
    while queue:
        _, current = heapq.heappop(queue)
        if current == goal:
            break
        visited.add(current)
        for neighbor in graph[current]:
            if neighbor not in visited:
                heapq.heappush(queue, (h(neighbor),
neighbor))
    return visited

# Example usage
graph = {
    ‚A‘: [‚B‘, ‚C‘],
    ‚B‘: [‚D‘, ‚E‘],
    ‚C‘: [‚F‘],
    ‚D‘: [],
    ‚E‘: [‚F‘],
    ‚F‘: []
}

def heuristic(node):
    H = {
        ‚A‘: 3,
        ‚B‘: 2,
        ‚C‘: 1,
        ‚D‘: 3,
        ‚E‘: 2,
        ‚F‘: 0
    }
    return H[node]
```

visited_nodes = greedy_best_first_search(graph, ‚A‘, ‚F‘, heuristic)
print(„Visited nodes:“, visited_nodes)

This Python code demonstrates Greedy Best-First Search in a simple graph. The heuristic function helps guide the search towards the goal.

17 Jump Search

Introduction and Historical Background

Jump Search, also known as block search, is a search algorithm for ordered lists. It's a relatively simple and straightforward algorithm that bridges the gap between linear search and binary search. The key idea behind Jump Search is to check fewer elements by jumping ahead by fixed steps.

Explanation and Theory

Conceptual Explanation:
Jump Search divides the list into smaller blocks and jumps through them to find the block that contains the target element. Once the appropriate block is found, a linear search is performed within that block. This approach significantly reduces the number of comparisons.

Mathematical Foundation:
The optimal block size to be jumped is where $\sqrt{n}$ is the size of the list. With this block size, the time complexity of Jump Search becomes $O(\sqrt{n})$, which is between $O(n)$ for linear search and $O(\log n)$ for binary search.

Use Cases and Applications

Real-World Applications:
Jump Search is particularly useful in situations where binary search is too resource-intensive, or when the data is too large for complete indexing. It's also used when you need a good balance between speed and simplicity in sorted lists or arrays.

Case Studies or Examples:
An example is searching through a large but sparsely populated address book, where binary search might be more intensive than necessary.

Python Implementation:

```python
import math

def jumpSearch(arr, x):
    n = len(arr)
    step = math.sqrt(n)

    prev = 0
    while arr[int(min(step, n)-1)] < x:
        prev = step
        step += math.sqrt(n)
        if prev >= n:
            return -1

    while arr[int(prev)] < x:
        prev += 1
        if prev == min(step, n):
            return -1

    if arr[int(prev)] == x:
        return int(prev)

    return -1

# Example usage
arr = [ 0, 1, 1, 2, 3, 5, 8, 13, 21, 34, 55, 89,
144]
x = 55
print(„Index:", jumpSearch(arr, x))
```

18 Interpolation Search

Introduction and Historical Background

Interpolation Search is an algorithm for searching for a specific key value in
an array that has been ordered by the values of the key. It is an improved va-
riant of binary search that is better suited for instances where the values in a
sorted array are uniformly distributed. Interpolation search was first propo-
sed in 1957 by W. W. Peterson, and it has been refined over the years.

Explanation and Theory

Conceptual Explanation:
Interpolation Search works on the principle of estimating the position of the target value within the sequence, based on the lowest and highest values in the array and the target value itself. It starts the search at the estimated position, narrowing the search range based on where the target lies in relation to this estimate.

Mathematical Foundation:
The key to its performance is how well the elements of the array are distributed. In the best case, the algorithm has a logarithmic time complexity, O(log log n), but in the worst case (for example, when the elements are not uniformly distributed), it can degrade to O(n).

Use Cases and Applications

Real-World Applications:
Interpolation Search is most effective for searching in large arrays with uniformly distributed values. It's particularly useful in applications where the data is large and a more efficient search than binary search is required.

Case Studies or Examples:
A practical example is in database query optimization where records are uniformly distributed and a quick search is essential.

Python Implementation:

```python
def interpolationSearch(arr, x):
    lo = 0
    hi = len(arr) - 1

    while lo <= hi and x >= arr[lo] and x <= arr[-hi]:
        if lo == hi:
            if arr[lo] == x:
                return lo
            return -1

        pos = lo + int(((float(hi - lo) / (arr[hi] - arr[lo])) * (x - arr[lo])))
```

```python
        if arr[pos] == x:
            return pos

        if arr[pos] < x:
            lo = pos + 1
        else:
            hi = pos - 1

    return -1

# Example usage
arr = [10, 12, 13, 16, 18, 19, 20, 21, 22, 23, 24,
33, 35, 42, 47]
x = 18
print(„Index of element:“, interpolationSearch(arr,
x))
```

This Python code demonstrates Interpolation Search, showcasing how it efficiently locates the position of a target value by estimating its position.

19 Kruskal's Minimum Spanning Tree Algorithm

Introduction and Historical Background

Kruskal's Minimum Spanning Tree Algorithm is a key algorithm in graph theory, used to find the minimum spanning tree for a connected, undirected graph. It was developed by Joseph Kruskal in 1956 and has since been a fundamental algorithm for network design and other applications.

Explanation and Theory

Conceptual Explanation:
Kruskal's algorithm approaches the problem by adding the shortest edge of the graph that doesn't form a cycle until all vertices are connected. This is done by organizing the edges in order of their weights and adding them to the spanning tree in this order, checking each time to ensure that a cycle is not formed.

Mathematical Foundation:
Kruskal's algorithm operates in O(E log E) time complexity, where E is the number of edges. This efficiency is mainly due to the sorting of the edges and the quick union-find operation for cycle detection.

Use Cases and Applications

Real-World Applications:
Kruskal's algorithm is used in designing network systems like telecommunications networks, electrical grids, and in computer networks for reducing the cost of wiring or cabling required for connecting various nodes.

Case Studies or Examples:
A practical example is in the layout of circuits in hardware design where a minimum wire length is desirable.

Python Implementation:

```python
class DisjointSet:
    def __init__(self, vertices):
        self.vertices = vertices
        self.parent = {v: v for v in vertices}
        self.rank = dict.fromkeys(vertices, 0)

    def find(self, item):
        if self.parent[item] == item:
            return item
        else:
            return self.find(self.parent[item])

    def union(self, x, y):
        rootx = self.find(x)
        rooty = self.find(y)
        if rootx != rooty:
            if self.rank[rootx] > self.rank[rooty]:
                self.parent[rooty] = rootx
            elif self.rank[rootx] < self.rank[rooty]:
                self.parent[rootx] = rooty
            else:
                self.parent[rooty] = rootx
```

```python
            self.rank[rootx] += 1

def kruskal(graph):
    edges = sorted(graph[‚edges‘], key=lambda e:
e[2])
    ds = DisjointSet(graph[‚vertices‘])
    mst = []
    for edge in edges:
        v1, v2, weight = edge
        if ds.find(v1) != ds.find(v2):
            mst.append(edge)
            ds.union(v1, v2)
    return mst

# Example usage
graph = {
    ‚vertices‘: [‚A‘, ‚B‘, ‚C‘, ‚D‘, ‚E‘, ‚F‘],
    ‚edges‘: set([
        (‚A‘, ‚B‘, 1),
        (‚A‘, ‚C‘, 3),
        (‚B‘, ‚C‘, 3),
        (‚B‘, ‚D‘, 1),
        (‚C‘, ‚D‘, 1),
        (‚C‘, ‚E‘, 5),
        (‚D‘, ‚E‘, 6),
        (‚E‘, ‚F‘, 2),
        (‚F‘, ‚A‘, 4),
    ])
}
print(„Minimum Spanning Tree:“, kruskal(graph))
```

This Python code demonstrates Kruskal's algorithm for finding the minimum spanning tree of a graph, using a disjoint-set data structure for efficient cycle detection.

20. Prim's Minimum Spanning Tree Algorithm

Introduction and Historical Background

Prim's Minimum Spanning Tree Algorithm is a classic algorithm in graph theory, developed by computer scientist Vojtěch Jarník in 1930 and later popularized by Robert C. Prim in 1957. It is used to find a minimum spanning tree for a weighted undirected graph, meaning it finds a subset of the edges that forms a tree that includes every vertex and where the total weight of all the edges in the tree is minimized.

Explanation and Theory

Conceptual Explanation:
Prim's algorithm works by growing the spanning tree from a starting position. It selects the cheapest edge from the tree to a vertex that is not yet in the tree and repeats this process until all vertices are included in the tree. At every step, it chooses the minimum weight edge that connects the tree to a new vertex.

Mathematical Foundation:
The time complexity of Prim's algorithm depends on the data structures used. With a simple implementation using a linear array, the complexity is $O(V^2)$, where V is the number of vertices. However, with a priority queue, it can be reduced to $O(E + V \log V)$, making it efficient for dense graphs.

Use Cases and Applications

Real-World Applications:
Prim's algorithm is used in network design, such as in the layout of roads, telecommunication networks, or electrical grids, where the goal is to minimize the cost of connecting all points in the network.

Case Studies or Examples:
A practical example is the design of a network of pipelines in the oil and gas industry, where the cost of laying pipelines over distances is to be minimized.

Python Implementation:

```python
import heapq

def prim(graph, start):
    mst, visited = [], set()
    edges = [(0, start, start)]
    while edges:
        weight, frm, to = heapq.heappop(edges)
```

```python
        if to not in visited:
            visited.add(to)
            mst.append((frm, to, weight))
            for next_node, weight in graph[to].
items():
                if next_node not in visited:
                    heapq.heappush(edges, (weight,
to, next_node))
    return mst

# Example usage
graph = {
    ‚A‘: {‚B‘: 4, ‚H‘: 8},
    ‚B‘: {‚A‘: 4, ‚C‘: 8, ‚H‘: 11},
    ‚C‘: {‚B‘: 8, ‚D‘: 7, ‚F‘: 4, ‚I‘: 2},
    ‚D‘: {‚C‘: 7, ‚E‘: 9, ‚F‘: 14},
    ‚E‘: {‚D‘: 9, ‚F‘: 10},
    ‚F‘: {‚C‘: 4, ‚D‘: 14, ‚E‘: 10, ‚G‘: 2},
    ‚G‘: {‚F‘: 2, ‚H‘: 1, ‚I‘: 6},
    ‚H‘: {‚A‘: 8, ‚B‘: 11, ‚G‘: 1, ‚I‘: 7},
    ‚I‘: {‚C‘: 2, ‚G‘: 6, ‚H‘: 7}
}
print(„Minimum Spanning Tree:“, prim(graph, ‚A‘))
```

This Python code demonstrates Prim's algorithm, showing how it constructs the minimum spanning tree by connecting the nearest unvisited vertex at each step.

21. Topological Sort

Introduction and Historical Background

Topological Sort is a linear ordering of vertices in a directed graph where for every directed edge from vertex uu to vertex vv, vertex uu comes before vv in the ordering. This concept is crucial in scenarios where certain tasks must precede others. It was first introduced in the early 20th century in the context of algebraic systems and has since been a fundamental concept in graph theory and computer science.

Explanation and Theory

Conceptual Explanation:
Topological Sorting of a graph is possible only if the graph is a Directed
Acyclic Graph (DAG), meaning it doesn't contain any cycles. The algorithm
works by repeatedly finding and removing a vertex with no incoming edges,
effectively „peeling off" layers of the graph.

Mathematical Foundation:
The time complexity of a Topological Sort is $O(V+E)O(V+E)$, where VV
is the number of vertices and EE is the number of edges in the graph. This
makes it efficient for analyzing dependencies among tasks.

Use Cases and Applications

Real-World Applications:
Topological Sorting is used in scheduling tasks, ordering of formula cell
evaluation in spreadsheets, logic synthesis, determining the order of compi-
lation tasks in makefiles, data serialization, and resolving symbol dependencies in linkers.

Case Studies or Examples:
A classic example is in project scheduling in construction or software development where certain tasks cannot begin until others are completed.

Python Implementation:

```python
from collections import deque

def topological_sort(graph):
    in_degree = { u : 0 for u in graph }
    for u in graph:
        for v in graph[u]:
            in_degree[v] += 1

    queue = deque()
    for u in in_degree:
        if in_degree[u] == 0:
            queue.appendleft(u)

    l = []
```

```python
    while queue:
        u = queue.pop()
        l.append(u)
        for v in graph[u]:
            in_degree[v] -= 1
            if in_degree[v] == 0:
                queue.appendleft(v)

    return l

# Example usage
graph = {
    ‚A‘: [‚C‘],
    ‚B‘: [‚C‘, ‚D‘],
    ‚C‘: [‚E‘],
    ‚D‘: [‚F‘],
    ‚E‘: [‚F‘],
    ‚F‘: []
}
order = topological_sort(graph)
print(„Topological Order:“, order)
```

This Python code demonstrates how Topological Sort orders vertices in a
Directed Acyclic Graph, ensuring that all directed edges point from a vertex
earlier in the order to a vertex later in the order.

22. Bellman-Ford Algorithm

Introduction and Historical Background

Bellman-Ford Algorithm is a graph algorithm that calculates the shortest
paths from a single source vertex to all other vertices in a weighted graph. It
was developed by Richard Bellman and Lester Ford Jr. in 1958. Unlike Dijkstra‘s algorithm, Bellman-Ford is capable of handling graphs with negative
weight edges, making it more versatile in certain scenarios.

Explanation and Theory

Conceptual Explanation:
The Bellman-Ford algorithm works by iteratively relaxing the edges of the

graph. The algorithm relaxes each edge by checking if the best known way to the destination vertex can be improved by taking the edge from the source vertex. It repeats this process for all edges in the graph for $V-1V-1$ iterations, where VV is the number of vertices in the graph.

Mathematical Foundation:
The time complexity of the Bellman-Ford algorithm is $O(V \cdot E)$, where V is the number of vertices and E is the number of edges. This makes it less efficient than Dijkstra's algorithm for graphs without negative weight edges but crucial for those with such edges.

Use Cases and Applications

Real-World Applications:
Bellman-Ford is used in network routing protocols like Routing Information Protocol (RIP) and in finding shortest path routing in scenarios where there may be negative path costs. It's also used in financial applications to detect negative cycles (indicating potential arbitrage opportunities).

Case Studies or Examples:
A practical application is in currency exchange, where the algorithm can help identify opportunities for arbitrage through currency exchanges that may result in a negative cycle.

Python Implementation:

```python
def bellman_ford(graph, source):
    distance = {vertex: float(‚infinity‘) for vertex
in graph}
    distance[source] = 0

    for _ in range(len(graph) - 1):
        for vertex in graph:
            for neighbour, weight in graph[vertex].
items():
                if distance[vertex] + weight < dis-
tance[neighbour]:
                    distance[neighbour] = distan-
ce[vertex] + weight

    for vertex in graph:
```

```python
        for neighbour, weight in graph[vertex].
items():
            if distance[vertex] + weight < distan-
ce[neighbour]:
                return „Negative weight cycle
found“

    return distance

# Example usage
graph = {
    ‚A‘: {‚B‘: -1, ‚C‘:  4},
    ‚B‘: {‚C‘:  3, ‚D‘:  2, ‚E‘:  2},
    ‚C‘: {},
    ‚D‘: {‚B‘:  1, ‚C‘:  5},
    ‚E‘: {‚D‘: -3}
}
print(„Shortest Paths:“, bellman_ford(graph,  ‚A‘))
```

This Python code illustrates the Bellman-Ford algorithm, showcasing its ability to handle graphs with negative weight edges and detect negative weight cycles.

23. Floyd-Warshall Algorithm

Introduction and Historical Background

Floyd-Warshall Algorithm is a classic algorithm in computer science for finding the shortest paths in a weighted graph with positive or negative edge weights (but no negative cycles). The algorithm was independently discovered by Robert Floyd and Stephen Warshall in the 1960s and is an example of dynamic programming.

Explanation and Theory

Conceptual Explanation:
The Floyd-Warshall algorithm compares all possible paths through the graph between each pair of vertices. It is able to do this with just a few operations for each pair of edges, making it efficient for computing the shortest paths in dense graphs. The key idea is to incrementally improve an estimate of the

shortest path between two vertices, until the estimate is optimal.

Mathematical Foundation:
The time complexity of the Floyd-Warshall algorithm is $O(V3)O(V3)$, where VV is the number of vertices in the graph. This cubic time complexity makes it less suitable for large graphs but very efficient for small to medium-sized graphs.

Use Cases and Applications

Real-World Applications:
The algorithm is used in scenarios where all pairs shortest paths are required. Applications include network routing, urban transportation planning, and in the computation of transitive closure in database systems.

Case Studies or Examples:
A practical application is in computing the shortest path in traffic networks, where finding the optimal route from all points to all other points is necessary.

Python Implementation:

```python
def floyd_warshall(graph):
    vertices = graph.keys()
    distance = {vertex: dict.fromkeys(vertices, flo-
at(,infinity')) for vertex in vertices}
    for vertex in vertices:
        distance[vertex][vertex] = 0
        for neighbour, weight in graph[vertex].
items():
            distance[vertex][neighbour] = weight

    for k in vertices:
        for i in vertices:
            for j in vertices:
                distance[i][j] = min(distance[i]
[j], distance[i][k] + distance[k][j])

    return distance

# Example usage
```

```python
graph = {
    ‚A‘: {‚B‘: 1, ‚C‘: 4},
    ‚B‘: {‚C‘: 2, ‚D‘: 2},
    ‚C‘: {‚D‘: 3},
    ‚D‘: {‚C‘: 1, ‚A‘: 7}
}
print(„Shortest Paths:“, floyd_warshall(graph))
```

This Python code demonstrates the Floyd-Warshall algorithm, showing how it calculates the shortest paths between every pair of vertices in the graph.

24. Johnson's Algorithm

Introduction and Historical Background

Johnson's Algorithm is a way to find the shortest paths between all pairs of vertices in a sparse, edge-weighted, directed graph. It was developed by Donald B. Johnson in 1977. This algorithm combines both Dijkstra's algorithm and the Bellman-Ford algorithm, effectively leveraging the strengths of both.

Explanation and Theory

Conceptual Explanation:
Johnson's Algorithm first uses the Bellman-Ford algorithm to reweight the edges to eliminate any negative weights. This step ensures the non-negativity of all edges, making it possible to use Dijkstra's algorithm. After reweighting, it applies Dijkstra's algorithm for each vertex to find the shortest paths from that vertex to all other vertices.

Mathematical Foundation:
The time complexity of Johnson's algorithm is $O(V2\log V+VE)O$, where V is the number of vertices and E is the number of edges. This makes it more efficient than the Floyd-Warshall algorithm for sparse graphs but less so for dense graphs.

Use Cases and Applications

Real-World Applications:
Johnson's algorithm is particularly useful in network analysis and routing, where the network is sparse but has some negative edge weights. It's also

used in scenarios requiring the computation of shortest paths between all pairs of nodes in a graph.

Case Studies or Examples:
An application could include traffic network analysis in a large city, where the goal is to find optimal routes between various points considering dynamic traffic conditions.

Python Implementation:

```python
import sys, heapq

def bellman_ford(graph, start):
    distance = {vertex: sys.maxsize for vertex in
graph}
    distance[start] = 0

    for _ in range(len(graph) - 1):
        for vertex in graph:
            for neighbor in graph[vertex]:
                if distance[vertex] + graph[vertex]
[neighbor] < distance[neighbor]:
                    distance[neighbor] = distance[-
vertex] + graph[vertex][neighbor]

    for vertex in graph:
        for neighbor in graph[vertex]:
            if distance[vertex] + graph[vertex]
[neighbor] < distance[neighbor]:
                return None
    return distance

def dijkstra(graph, start):
    distances = {vertex: float(,infinity') for vertex
in graph}
    distances[start] = 0
    pq = [(0, start)]

    while pq:
        current_distance, current_vertex = heapq.
heappop(pq)
```

```python
        if current_distance > distances[current_
vertex]:
            continue

        for neighbor, weight in graph[current_ver-
tex].items():
            distance = current_distance + weight

            if distance < distances[neighbor]:
                distances[neighbor] = distance
                heapq.heappush(pq, (distance, neig-
hbor))

    return distances

def johnson(graph):
    new_graph = graph.copy()
    new_graph[‚Q‘] = {v: 0 for v in graph}
    h = bellman_ford(new_graph, ‚Q‘)
    if h is None:
        return None

    for u in graph:
        for v in graph[u]:
            graph[u][v] += h[u] - h[v]

    distance = {u: {v: sys.maxsize for v in graph}
for u in graph}
    for u in graph:
        dist = dijkstra(graph, u)
        for v in graph:
            distance[u][v] = dist[v] + h[v] - h[u]

    return distance

# Example usage
graph = {
    ‚A‘: {‚B‘: 1,  ‚C‘: 4},
    ‚B‘: {‚C‘: 2, ‚D‘: 2},
    ‚C‘: {‚D‘: 3},
```

```python
    ‚D‘: {‚C‘: 1, ‚A‘: 7}
}
print(„Shortest Paths:“, johnson(graph))
```

This Python code outlines the Johnson's algorithm, showing how it combines Bellman-Ford and Dijkstra's algorithms for efficient shortest path calculations in sparse graphs.

25. Tarjan's Algorithm for Strongly Connected Components

Introduction and Historical Background

Tarjan's Algorithm, developed by Robert Tarjan in 1972, is a classic algorithm in graph theory for finding the strongly connected components of a directed graph. A strongly connected component (SCC) of a directed graph is a maximal set of vertices where each vertex is reachable from every other vertex in the set.

Explanation and Theory

Conceptual Explanation:
Tarjan's Algorithm uses depth-first search (DFS) to explore the graph and efficiently find SCCs by keeping track of the nodes visited and assigning each node a unique index, which plays a role similar to a timestamp. It identifies SCCs based on the discovery times of the vertices and a property known as „low-link values.“

Mathematical Foundation:
The time complexity of Tarjan's Algorithm is $O(V+E)$, where V is the number of vertices and E is the number of edges. This efficiency is due to the algorithm's single pass over the graph.

Use Cases and Applications

Real-World Applications:
SCCs are crucial in many applications, including analyzing networks, circuit testing, and in programming where dependencies exist among components. They are also used in the theoretical underpinning of many algorithms and

applications in computer science.

Case Studies or Examples:
An example is in software modularization, where understanding SCCs can help identify tightly coupled components and improve the design for better maintainability and scalability.

Python Implementation:

```python
def tarjan(graph):
    index_counter = [0]
    stack = []
    lowlinks = {}
    index = {}
    result = []

    def strongconnect(node):
        index[node] = index_counter[0]
        lowlinks[node] = index_counter[0]
        index_counter[0] += 1
        stack.append(node)

        for successor in graph[node]:
            if successor not in index:
                strongconnect(successor)
                lowlinks[node] = min(lowlinks[no-
de], lowlinks[successor])
            elif successor in stack:
                lowlinks[node] = min(lowlinks[no-
de], index[successor])

        if lowlinks[node] == index[node]:
            connected_component = []

            while True:
                successor = stack.pop()
                connected_component.append(succes-
sor)
                if successor == node:
                    break
            result.append(connected_component)
```

```python
    for node in graph:
        if node not in index:
            strongconnect(node)

    return result

# Example usage
graph = {
    'A': ['B'],
    'B': ['C', 'E', 'F'],
    'C': ['D', 'G'],
    'D': ['C', 'H'],
    'E': ['A', 'F'],
    'F': ['G'],
    'G': ['F'],
    'H': ['D', 'G']
}
print("Strongly connected components:", tar-
jan(graph))
```

This Python code demonstrates Tarjan's Algorithm, showcasing how it effectively identifies strongly connected components in a directed graph using depth-first search.

26. Fibonacci Series (with Memoization)

Introduction and Historical Background

Fibonacci Series is a sequence where each number is the sum of the two preceding ones, usually starting with 0 and 1. This series has been known to mathematicians for centuries and appears in different areas of mathematics and science. The use of memoization in computing the Fibonacci series, a technique of dynamic programming, significantly optimizes its calculation.

Explanation and Theory

Conceptual Explanation:
In the Fibonacci series, each term is the sum of the previous two terms:
$F(n)=F(n-1)+F(n-2)F(n)=F(n-1)+F(n-2)$ with base cases $F(0)=0F(0)=0$

and $F(1)=1$F(1)=1. The naive recursive implementation is inefficient due to redundant calculations. Memoization optimizes it by storing and reusing previously computed results, thereby reducing the number of calculations.

Mathematical Foundation:
The time complexity of the naive recursive approach is exponential, O(2n). However, with memoization, it drops to O(n), as each number in the series is calculated only once.

Use Cases and Applications

Real-World Applications:
The Fibonacci series is used in various fields, including computer science, mathematics, economics, and even in biological settings (e.g., modeling population growth). In programming, it's often used as an introductory problem for learning recursion and dynamic programming.

Case Studies or Examples:
A typical example is the estimation of time complexity in algorithm analysis and the teaching of recursion and memoization concepts in computer science courses.

Python Implementation:

```python
def fibonacci(n, memo={}):
    if n in memo:
        return memo[n]
    if n <= 1:
        return n
    memo[n] = fibonacci(n - 1, memo) + fibonacci(n - 2, memo)
    return memo[n]


# Example usage
n = 10
print(f"Fibonacci of {n}:", fibonacci(n))
```

This Python code demonstrates the Fibonacci series using memoization, highlighting how redundant calculations are avoided, thus optimizing the process.

27 Knapsack Problem

Introduction and Historical Background

Knapsack Problem is a problem in combinatorial optimization: given a set of items, each with a weight and a value, determine the number of each item to include in a collection so that the total weight is less than or equal to a given limit and the total value is as large as possible. This problem arises naturally in many contexts and is a fundamental problem in the study of algorithms and complexity.

Explanation and Theory

Conceptual Explanation:
The Knapsack Problem can be approached in several ways, but one common method is using dynamic programming. The idea is to build a table dp[i][w] which represents the maximum value that can be attained with weight less than or equal to w using items up to i. The algorithm then iteratively computes the entries of this table.

Mathematical Foundation:
The complexity of the Knapsack Problem using dynamic programming is $O(nW)$, where n is the number of items and W is the capacity of the knapsack. This makes the problem solvable in pseudo-polynomial time.

Use Cases and Applications

Real-World Applications:
The Knapsack Problem is used in resource allocation where the costs and values of resources are to be optimized. This includes applications in finance, resource allocation, and in the field of logistics.

Case Studies or Examples:
An example is in budgeting, such as maximizing the value of purchased products while staying within a budget limit.

Python Implementation:

```python
def knapSack(W, wt, val, n):
    K = [[0 for x in range(W + 1)] for x in range(n
+ 1)]

    for i in range(n + 1):
        for w in range(W + 1):
            if i == 0 or w == 0:
                K[i][w] = 0
            elif wt[i-1] <= w:
                K[i][w] = max(val[i-1] + K[i-1][w-
wt[i-1]], K[i-1][w])
            else:
                K[i][w] = K[i-1][w]

    return K[n][W]

# Example usage
val = [60, 100, 120]
wt = [10, 20, 30]
W = 50
n = len(val)
print(knapSack(W, wt, val, n))
```

This Python code implements the 0/1 Knapsack Problem using dynamic programming, demonstrating how to achieve the optimal combination of items within the given weight limit.

28 Longest Common Subsequence (LCS)

Introduction and Historical Background

Longest Common Subsequence (LCS) is a classic problem in computer science and combinatorial optimization. It involves finding the longest subsequence common to two (or more) sequences. LCS has applications in numerous fields, including bioinformatics, linguistics, and in the diff tools used in software version control systems.

Explanation and Theory

Conceptual Explanation:
The LCS problem can be solved using dynamic programming. The approach
involves creating a table dpdp where $dp[i][j]dp[i][j]$ stores the length of the
LCS of the sequences up to ii-th and jj-th element of each sequence respecti-
vely. The algorithm fills this table based on the comparison of elements of the
sequences.

Mathematical Foundation:
The time complexity of the LCS problem using dynamic programming
is O(mn), where m and n are the lengths of the two sequences. Although
computationally expensive for very long sequences, this approach is quite
efficient for moderate-sized sequences.

Use Cases and Applications

Real-World Applications:
LCS is used in text comparison, such as finding similarities between texts in
plagiarism detection software, and in bioinformatics for DNA and protein
sequence analysis. It's also used in the implementation of diff utilities for
version control systems.

Case Studies or Examples:
An example is in version control systems like Git, where the LCS algorithm
helps in identifying changes between different versions of files.

Python Implementation:

```python
def lcs(X, Y):
    m = len(X)
    n = len(Y)
    dp = [[0] * (n+1) for i in range(m+1)]

    for i in range(m+1):
        for j in range(n+1):
            if i == 0 or j == 0:
                dp[i][j] = 0
            elif X[i-1] == Y[j-1]:
                dp[i][j] = dp[i-1][j-1] + 1
            else:
```

```python
            dp[i][j] = max(dp[i-1][j], dp[i][j-1])

    return dp[m][n]

# Example usage
X = „AGGTAB"
Y = „GXTXAYB"
print(„Length of LCS is", lcs(X, Y))
```

This Python code implements the LCS algorithm, illustrating how to compute the length of the longest common subsequence of two strings.

29 Longest Increasing Subsequence (LIS)

Introduction and Historical Background

Longest Increasing Subsequence (LIS) is a classic problem in computer science and combinatorial optimization. The goal is to find the longest subsequence of a given sequence in which the elements are in sorted order, strictly increasing, and not necessarily contiguous. This problem has applications in various fields, including mathematics and computer science.

Explanation and Theory

Conceptual Explanation:
The LIS problem can be solved using dynamic programming. The idea is to maintain an array dpdp where dp[i]stores the length of the longest increasing subsequence ending at index i. For each element in the array, the algorithm finds the length of the LIS ending with that element by looking at all previous elements that are smaller and adding one to the maximum length found.

Mathematical Foundation:
The time complexity of the LIS problem using dynamic programming is $O(n2)$, where nn is the length of the input sequence. Each element of the array is compared with all other elements that precede it.

Use Cases and Applications

Real-World Applications:
LIS is used in data analysis for understanding and extracting meaningful sequences from larger datasets. It also has applications in fields like bioinformatics for sequence alignment and analysis.

Case Studies or Examples:
An example of its application is in analyzing trends in time series data, where identifying long increasing trends can be crucial for predictions and decision-making.

Python Implementation:

```python
def lis(arr):
    n = len(arr)
    lis = [1] * n

    for i in range (1, n):
        for j in range(0, i):
            if arr[i] > arr[j] and lis[i] < lis[j] + 1:
                lis[i] = lis[j] + 1

    return max(lis)

# Example usage
arr = [10, 22, 9, 33, 21, 50, 41, 60, 80]
print(„Length of LIS is", lis(arr))
```

This Python code illustrates the LIS algorithm, showing how to find the length of the longest increasing subsequence in an array of numbers.

30 Coin Change Problem

Introduction and Historical Background

Coin Change Problem is a classic problem in computer science and combinatorial optimization. The problem is to find the number of ways to make change for a particular amount of money, given a set of coins with different denominations. It is a problem often used to introduce the concept of dynamic programming.

Explanation and Theory

Conceptual Explanation:
The Coin Change Problem can be solved using dynamic programming by building a table dp[]dp[] in a bottom-up manner. dp[i]will be storing the number of solutions for value i. The idea is to build the solution of dp[i] from smaller values of i using the coin denominations available.

Mathematical Foundation:
The time complexity of the Coin Change Problem using dynamic programming is $O(m \times n)$, where m is the amount and n is the number of coin denominations. The algorithm efficiently computes the solution by reusing previously computed values.

Use Cases and Applications

Real-World Applications:
The Coin Change Problem has applications in finance, such as in ATM machines for dispensing a certain amount using a minimal number of bills or coins. It's also relevant in vending machines and cash register systems for providing change.

Case Studies or Examples:
An example is in electronic payment systems, where the goal is to minimize the number of coins and bills returned as change in a transaction.

Python Implementation:

```python
def coinChange(coins, amount):
    dp = [float(,inf')] * (amount + 1)
    dp[0] = 0

    for i in range(1, amount + 1):
        for coin in coins:
            if i - coin >= 0:
                dp[i] = min(dp[i], dp[i - coin] +
1)
```

```python
    return dp[amount] if dp[amount] != float(‚inf')
else -1

# Example usage
coins = [1, 2, 5]
amount = 11
print(„Minimum coins needed:", coinChange(coins,
amount))
```

This Python code solves the Coin Change Problem, demonstrating how to find the minimum number of coins that you need to make up a given amount.

www.ingramcontent.com/pod-product-compliance
Lightning Source LLC
Chambersburg PA
CBHW052235150726
48002CB00003B/1449